Brands We Know

Nike

By Sara Green

Bellwether Media • Minneapolis, MN

Jump into the cockpit and take flight with *Pilot books.* Your journey will take you on high-energy adventures as you learn about all that is wild, weird, fascinating, and fun!

This edition first published in 2015 by Bellwether Media, Inc.

No part of this publication may be reproduced in whole or in part without written permission of the publisher.
For information regarding permission, write to Bellwether Media, Inc.,
Attention: Permissions Department,
5357 Penn Avenue South, Minneapolis, MN 55419.

Library of Congress Cataloging-in-Publication Data

Green, Sara, 1964-
 Nike / by Sara Green.
   pages cm. -- (Pilot: Brands We Know)
 Includes bibliographical references and index.
 Summary: "Engaging images accompany information about Nike, Inc.
The combination of high-interest subject matter and narrative text is
intended for students in grades 3 through 7"-- Provided by publisher.
 Audience: 7-12.
 Audience: Grades 3-7.
 ISBN 978-1-62617-210-4 (hardcover : alk. paper)
1. Nike (Firm)--History--Juvenile literature. 2. Sporting goods
industry--United States--History--Juvenile literature. 3. Footwear
industry--United States--History--Juvenile literature. 4. Athletic
shoes--History--Juvenile literature. I. Title.
 HD9992.U54N5534 2015
 338.7'68536--dc23
                        2014043850

Printed in the United States of America, North Mankato, MN.

Table of Contents

What Is Nike?

Sports are an important part of many people's lives. Some athletes like to compete individually. Others prefer to be part of a team. No matter the sport, Nike has probably made shoes, clothes, or equipment for it.

Nike, Inc. is an American sportswear company. It is the world's largest **manufacturer** of athletic shoes, clothes, and equipment. The company **headquarters** are in Beaverton, Oregon. However, Nike sells products in more than 180 countries. Nike is one of the most widely known **brands** on Earth. People all over the world are familiar with Nike's famous **slogan**, "Just Do It." Most recognize the brand's Swoosh **logo**. In 2014, the company was worth more than $65 billion. This makes Nike one of the most valuable brands on the planet!

By the Numbers

48,000
employees
worldwide

more than
750
Nike retail stores
worldwide

more than
$2.7 billion
spent in 2013 on advertising
and endorsements

$27 billion
in sales in 2013

$90 million
reportedly paid to Nike's
highest paid athlete,
Michael Jordan, in 2013

Nike, Inc. headquarters

Blue Ribbon Sports

Nike began with a man's search for a better running shoe. In 1961, Phil Knight was a graduate student at Stanford University in California. He was assigned to write a paper about starting a small business. Phil's love of running inspired his paper topic. In college, he ran track at the University of Oregon. Phil created a plan to **import** running shoes from Japan. He would sell the shoes in the United States. After Phil graduated from Stanford in 1962, he put his idea into practice.

Phil traveled to Japan and introduced himself to **executives** at the Onitsuka company. It made an athletic shoe called the Tiger. Phil claimed to be the head of an import company named Blue Ribbon Sports. He asked for permission to sell Tiger shoes. The executives agreed. However, Phil had a problem. Blue Ribbon Sports was not a real company yet.

Onitsuka Tiger ··········

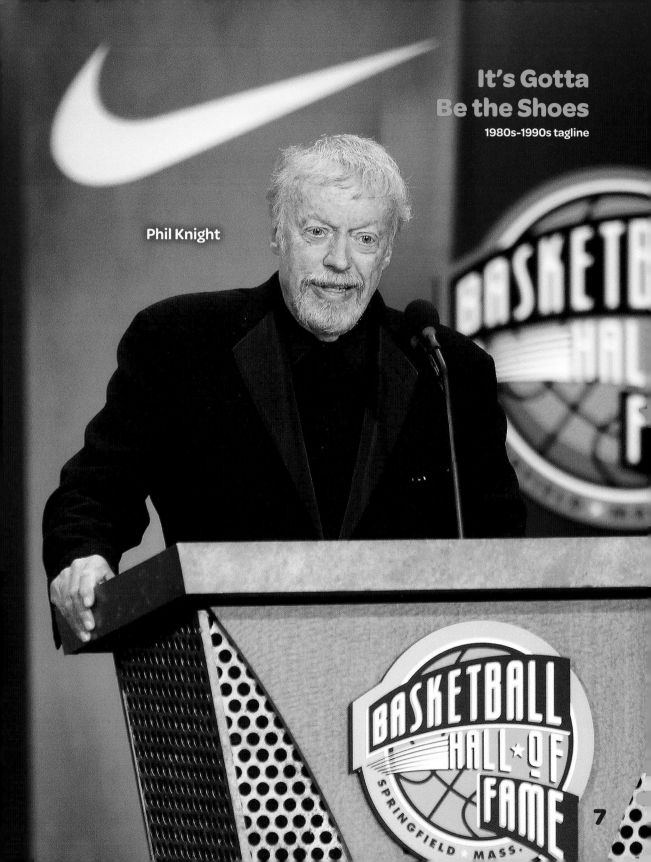

It's Gotta
Be the Shoes

1980s-1990s tagline

Phil Knight

My Better Is Better
Than Your Better

2000s tagline

Bill Bowerman

Phil Knight

What a Deal!
Carolyn Davidson was paid
just $35 for designing
the Swoosh logo.

Back home, Phil met with Bill Bowerman, his University of Oregon track coach. Bill agreed to help Phil start Blue Ribbon Sports. Soon, they received their first shipment of Tiger running shoes from Japan. Phil traveled to track meets in the **Pacific Northwest**. He sold the Tigers from his car. Runners liked the lightweight, inexpensive shoes. In 1964, Phil made more than $3,000 selling the shoes. Sales continued to climb. In 1966, the company outgrew selling from cars. It moved to a storefront in Santa Monica, California.

After a few years, Phil and Bill began to have problems with Onitsuka. It was time for the two companies to part ways. Phil and Bill created their own brand. An employee named Jeff Johnson suggested the name Nike, after the Greek goddess of victory. An art student named Carolyn Davidson designed the Swoosh logo for the brand. In 1971, Blue Ribbon Sports released a soccer cleat called the Nike. It was the first with the Nike name and the Swoosh logo.

Greek goddess of victory

The Growth of Nike

Bill liked to tinker with shoe designs. His goal was to make a comfortable running shoe with great **traction**. A waffle iron gave him an idea. Bill poured liquid rubber into the waffle iron and made a **sole**. He used waffle soles to make running shoes bearing the Nike name. Bill also coached the 1972 U.S. Olympic Track Team. Many of his runners wore the new shoes at the U.S. Olympic Trials. One was a record holder named Steve Prefontaine. His success in the trials made the Nike name famous.

waffle shoe

Run, Forrest, Run!
In the movie *Forrest Gump*, Forrest wore Nike Cortez shoes when he ran across the United States.

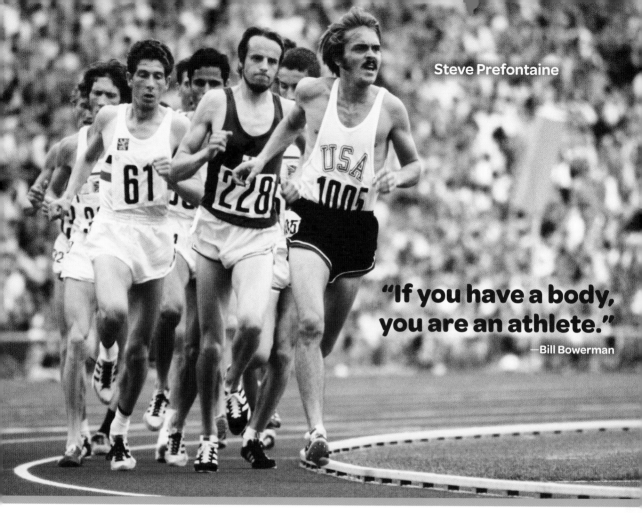

Steve Prefontaine

"If you have a body, you are an athlete."
—Bill Bowerman

The company grew rapidly. It continued to seek ways to improve its shoes. In 1977, a man named Frank Rudy created the first soles filled with gas. The company called this Nike Air cushioning. In 1978, the Nike Tailwind **debuted**. This running shoe was the first to have Air-soles. Around this time, Phil and Bill decided it was time for a new company name. In 1978, the men renamed their company Nike, Inc.

Phil wanted to sell more shoes, but he did not like to **advertise**. He came up with a better idea. He began to pay top athletes to **endorse** Nike shoes. Over time, Nike found great success with this method. In 1984, the company signed a basketball player named Michael Jordan. He endorsed a red and black basketball sneaker called the Air Jordan. Television commercials showed Michael soaring through the air and slam-dunking basketballs in Air Jordans. Within a year, the Air Jordan was a top-selling item. By 1986, Nike sales reached $1 billion. Nike, Inc. was the number one shoe manufacturer in the world.

Michael Jordan

A Superstar Sneaker

At first, the NBA banned the Air Jordan shoe. It did not match the league's dress code. However, the ban helped make the shoe more famous. Customers wanted it even more.

Mia Hamm

Roger Federer

United States men's national soccer team

LeBron James

Brazilian men's national soccer team

Over time, many famous athletes have endorsed Nike products. Mia Hamm, Roger Federer, and LeBron James are top athletes who wear the Nike brand. Entire teams also endorse the brand. They include the United States, Brazilian, and English men's national soccer teams.

In 1988, Nike, Inc. introduced the slogan "Just Do It." This short, simple phrase was an instant hit. Soon, it became part of all Nike ads and television commercials. Today, "Just Do It" remains one of the most successful slogans of all time. Nike is also known for other successful ads. "Bo Knows" was an ad from 1989 to 1990 starring Bo Jackson. The football and baseball star endorsed **cross-training** shoes. In 1995, Nike released its "If You Let Me Play" ads. In these, girls talked about the benefits of playing sports.

Creative ads have helped Nike achieve great success. However, not everyone has always approved of the company. Nike uses factories in Asia to make its products. Many laborers work in unsafe conditions for low wages. People have protested these practices. As a result, Nike, Inc. raised wages and improved safety. Unfortunately, problems remain. Nike continues to seek solutions.

Nike Endorsements

Athlete	Country	Sport
Drew Brees	United States	Football
Gracie Gold	United States	Figure Skating
Mia Hamm	United States	Soccer
LeBron James	United States	Basketball
Derek Jeter	United States	Baseball
Shawn Johnson	United States	Gymnastics
Michael Jordan	United States	Basketball
Julia Mancuso	United States	Alpine Skiing
Rafael Nadal	Spain	Tennis
Cristiano Ronaldo	Portugal	Soccer
Maria Sharapova	Russia	Tennis
Michelle Wie	United States	Golf
Serena Williams	United States	Tennis

A Technology Leader

Nike, Inc. is a leader in sports equipment research. In 2000, the company started its Techlab division. It tests products to help athletes perform better. One popular **innovation** is a knitted running shoe called the Flyknit. This lightweight shoe fits the foot like a second skin. Some basketball players wear the Hyperdunk shoe. It is made from a strong, lightweight fabric called Flywire. The Hyperdunk is among the best basketball shoes available today.

Flyknit

Hyperdunk

Going to the Extreme

In 1996, Nike created a line for extreme sports. Its products include hiking boots and snowboarding clothing.

FuelBand

Nike Vapor golf clubs

For golf, Techlab developed more **efficient** clubs and balls. Golfers can have stronger strokes and farther flying balls. Nike has also introduced a baseball glove that does not need to be broken in. Another popular invention is a wristband called the FuelBand. It tracks and records daily movement. With inventions such as these, Nike helps athletes achieve great things.

Making the World
a Better Place

In 1993, Nike, Inc. introduced the Reuse-A-Shoe program. It recycles athletic shoes and grinds them up into material. This is used to make running tracks, playgrounds, and basketball courts. In 2005, the company launched an environmentally friendly line of shoes called Nike Considered. Shoe materials are **nontoxic** and making them produces little waste. The company now uses these practices in all its products. It also aims to make its products recyclable. Some clothing is made with recycled plastic bottles. This has kept more than two billion bottles out of landfills.

Nike, Inc. also helps people through a **charitable** organization called the Nike **Foundation**. Its goal is to end **poverty** around the world. In 2008, it launched a program called The Girl Effect. This program promotes education and health for girls in poorer countries. It **empowers** them to make positive changes in their communities. Through this program and others, the foundation helps brighten people's futures all over the world.

Reuse-A-Shoe

Nike Timeline

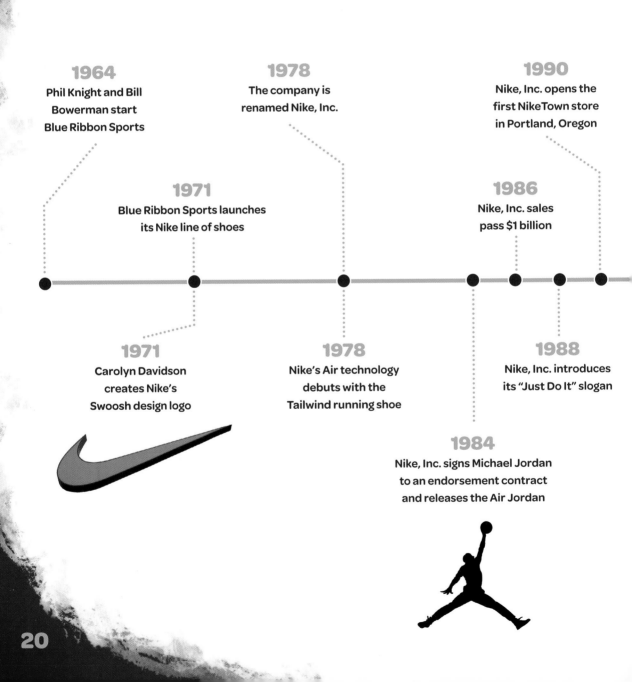

1964
Phil Knight and Bill Bowerman start Blue Ribbon Sports

1978
The company is renamed Nike, Inc.

1990
Nike, Inc. opens the first NikeTown store in Portland, Oregon

1971
Blue Ribbon Sports launches its Nike line of shoes

1986
Nike, Inc. sales pass $1 billion

1971
Carolyn Davidson creates Nike's Swoosh design logo

1978
Nike's Air technology debuts with the Tailwind running shoe

1988
Nike, Inc. introduces its "Just Do It" slogan

1984
Nike, Inc. signs Michael Jordan to an endorsement contract and releases the Air Jordan

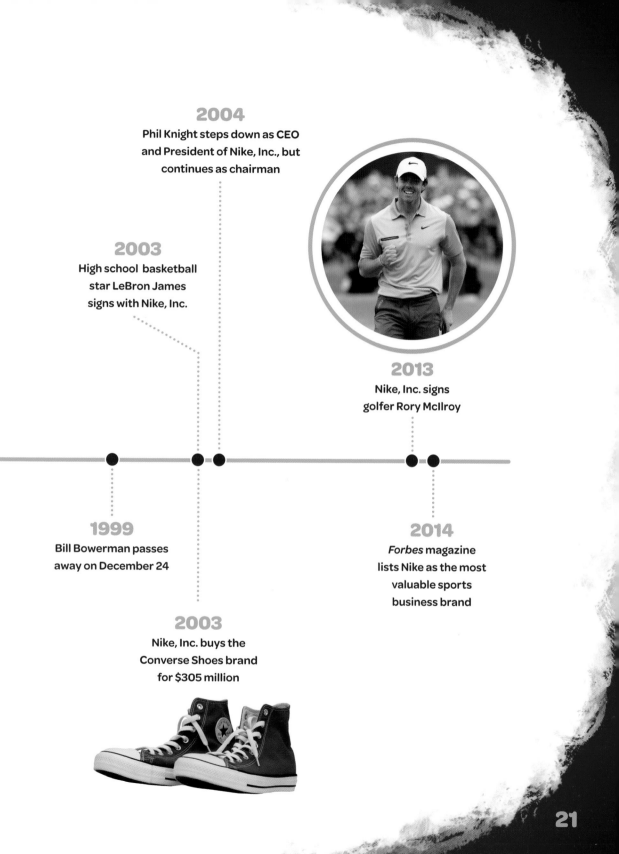

2004

Phil Knight steps down as CEO and President of Nike, Inc., but continues as chairman

2003

High school basketball star LeBron James signs with Nike, Inc.

2013

Nike, Inc. signs golfer Rory McIlroy

1999

Bill Bowerman passes away on December 24

2014

Forbes magazine lists Nike as the most valuable sports business brand

2003

Nike, Inc. buys the Converse Shoes brand for $305 million

Glossary

advertise—to announce or promote something to get people to buy it

brands—categories of products all made by the same company

charitable—helping others in need

cross-training—training in two or more sports

debuted—was introduced for the first time

efficient—performing in the best possible way with the least amount of effort

empowers—makes somebody stronger and more confident

endorse—to publicly say you like or use a product in exchange for money

executives—leaders of a company

foundation—an institution that provides funds to charitable organizations

headquarters—a company's main office

import—to bring products from one country to another

innovation—a new method, product, or idea

logo—a symbol or design that identifies a brand or product

manufacturer—a company that makes items for people to use

nontoxic—not poisonous

Pacific Northwest—the region of the United States that includes Oregon and Washington

poverty—the state of being poor

slogan—a short, memorable phrase used in advertising

sole—bottom surface of a shoe

traction—grip of a shoe on a surface

To Learn More

AT THE LIBRARY

Frederick, Shane. *The Kids' Guide to Sports Media*. North Mankato, Minn.: Capstone Press, 2014.

Frisch, Aaron. *The Story of Nike*. Mankato, Minn.: Creative Education, 2009.

Gifford, Clive. *Track and Field*. New York, N.Y.: PowerKids Press, 2009.

ON THE WEB

Learning more about Nike is as easy as 1, 2, 3.

1. Go to www.factsurfer.com.

2. Enter "Nike" into the search box.

3. Click the "Surf" button and you will see a list of related web sites.

With factsurfer.com, finding more information is just a click away.

Index